THE BIRTH
OF CHRIST

THE BIRTH OF CHRIST

The Biblical Significance of Christmas

J. V. Fesko

Reformation Heritage Books
Grand Rapids, Michigan

The Birth of Christ
© 2022 by J. V. Fesko

Reformation Heritage Books
3070 29th St. SE, Grand Rapids, MI 49512
616-977-0889
orders@heritagebooks.org
www.heritagebooks.org

Printed in the United States of America
22 23 24 25 26 27/10 9 8 7 6 5 4 3 2 1

Library of Congress Cataloging-in-Publication Data

Names: Fesko, J. V., 1970- author.
Title: The birth of Christ : the Biblical significance of Christmas / J.V. Fesko.
Description: Grand Rapids, Michigan : Reformation Heritage Books, [2022] |
    Includes bibliographical references.
Identifiers: LCCN 2022024009 (print) | LCCN 2022024010 (ebook) |
    ISBN 9781601789570 (paperback) | ISBN 9781601789587 (epub)
Subjects: LCSH: Jesus Christ—Nativity—Biblical teaching. | Christmas—
    Biblical teaching. | Jesus Christ—Nativity—Meditations. | Christmas—
    Meditations. | BISAC: RELIGION / Holidays / Christmas & Advent |
    RELIGION / Christian Living / General
Classification: LCC BT315.3 .F47 2022 (print) | LCC BT315.3 (ebook) |
    DDC 232.92—dc23/eng/20220615
LC record available at https://lccn.loc.gov/2022024009
LC ebook record available at https://lccn.loc.gov/2022024010

For additional Reformed literature, request a free book list from Reformation Heritage Books at the above regular or email address.

Dedicated to

Pastor Allen Stanton

and the saints at
Pinehaven Presbyterian Church
Clinton, Mississippi

Contents

Preface

This small devotional book contains a number of Christmas messages that I have preached over the last fifteen years, and my goal has always been the same: to ensure that the church does not lose sight of the real meaning of the birth of Christ. I present these messages in this small book in the hopes that it will serve as a booster shot year-round, but especially at Christmastime, so that Christ always fills the horizon of our faith. One of the chapters, "O Come, O Come, Emmanuel," originally began as a sermon but was later published in the December 2008 issue of *New Horizons*, the denominational magazine of the Orthodox Presbyterian Church.

I am grateful to Reformation Heritage Books for their continued partnership over the years in publishing my writing. Thank you to Joel Beeke, David Woollin, and Jay Collier. I am also thankful to my family, who listened to me preach and later read aloud a number of these chapters, and especially to my wife, who offered me helpful feedback and suggestions.

I dedicate this book to the saints of Pinehaven Presbyterian Church in Clinton, Mississippi, a dear congregation of God's people. The Lord granted me the privilege to serve them by preaching during a challenging season: the virus, riots, storms, political unrest. More personally during this tumultuous time, Pinehaven's pastor, Rev. Allen Stanton, was diagnosed with and treated for brain cancer. May they look back upon these times and see the sustenance God provided and that our God did not allow the darkness of the valley of the shadow of death to overwhelm them. May we all remember our God is faithful. He sent His only begotten Son to save us, and He is with us through the presence of His Spirit.

Introduction

Each year as fall gives way to winter, the air grows cold, leaves drop from the trees, and people begin to look forward to the end of the year and the Christmas holiday season. Stores put up displays, tractor trailers loaded with Christmas trees arrive at shopping clubs, people decorate their homes, and the familiar songs of Christmas play on satellite radio and in the retail stores that we frequent. Children mark their calendars, fill their Amazon wish lists, and eagerly keep watch over the Christmas tree to see what gifts begin to appear. It is a fun time of the year, and in the midst of these Christmas activities, our surrounding culture gives a nod to the fact that the holiday is supposed to be about Jesus. We can probably think of different quotes that are invoked to remind people of the real meaning of Christmas: "Jesus is the reason for the season." Or, "The beauty of Christmas is not in the presents but in His presence." In the ongoing culture wars in the West, many secularists are aware of the religious nature of Christmas and have tried to replace the term *Christmas* with *holiday*. They see *Christ* in the term *Christmas* and therefore try to eliminate the word altogether. But the question we have to ask ourselves is, How Christian is our celebration of Christmas? During the Christmas holidays, how much do we meditate upon the significance of the birth of Christ and all that means?

Conversely, do we get lost in all the seasonal cheer and reduce our celebration of Christ's birth to a few Christmas hymns and maybe a Christmas church service?

Part of the challenge of Christmas is ensuring that the truth of the gospel does not get flooded in a tsunami of commercialism, sentimentalism, and syncretism. Make no mistake about it, most retail stores have no interest in promoting the gospel of Christ. They worship at the altar of one god, Mammon. Retailers want to see their ledgers in the black, and December is typically when they make the bulk of their profits. Marketing is slick, attractive, and pulls at our heart strings. Who, after all, does not want to make people happy by giving them gifts? Who does not want to be made happy by receiving gifts? Retailers therefore bombard us with ads, links, emails, and displays so that we will buy, buy, buy. Merchants use Jesus as a marketing tool to achieve their sales goals. One advertisement I recently saw shows a scene where the infant Jesus lies in his manger surrounded by Mary, Joseph, the shepherds, and a cow—Jesus wears a small Santa suit.

Such marketing is an effort to evoke a sentimental response. We associate Christmas with Jesus and many have fond childhood memories of opening gifts on Christmas morning. We may want to relive those memories and pass them on to our children and, yes, of course, also remember that Jesus is the reason for the season. But what happens when our emotions and feelings collide with biblical truths of Christmas that most people ignore or seldom invoke? The Christmas hymn "The First Noel," for example, recounts the angel's announcement of Christ's birth to the shepherds:

The first Noel the angel did say
Was to certain poor shepherds in fields as they lay,
In fields where they lay keeping their sheep,
On a cold winter's night that was so deep.

The hymn's lyrics are fine as far as they go, but the selective use of Luke's narrative omits important facts that likely do not stoke the embers of our emotions. The angel had to tell the shepherds not to fear—angels are terrifying beings (Luke 2:10). The angel also announced the birth of the Savior, "Christ the Lord" (v. 11). How many people in the broader culture who observe Christmas recognize that the Christ, the Lord's Anointed, will take the unbelieving nations and "break them with a rod of iron" and "dash them to pieces like a potter's vessel" (Ps. 2:9)?

One of the biggest problems during the Christmas season is syncretism—combining biblical teaching with various false beliefs. Syncretism was a constant threat to Israel in the Old Testament and to the New Testament church. Israelites thought they could combine the worship of God with Baal, and some New Testament Christians tried to synthesize Christianity with early forms of Docetism, the belief that Jesus was not actually literally and physically incarnate as a man but only appeared as a spirit or apparition. The dangers of syncretism always abound, and this is especially true at Christmas. When satellite radio stations play Christmas music, they broadcast Christmas hymns and carols, "Silent Night" and "Frosty the Snowman," as if they were both about the same thing. Christians are aware of this and try to do what they can to "redeem" the holiday by replacing secular Christmas practices with Christianized ones. One such tradition is the Elf on the Shelf, an elf doll that keeps watch during the day and reports back to Santa each night about who was naughty or nice; parents secretly move the elf each night, and children discover the next morning where the elf has reappeared. One company offers a Christian alternative: Fun with the Son!, a Christmas game of hide-and-seek with a Jesus doll. While the effort to protect the sanctity of Christmas is noble and desirable, should we not first stop and ask whether making Jesus dolls is biblically allowable? Second, does Fun with the Son send the unintended message that our Savior merely reports our good and bad deeds back to the Father rather than save us because this is how you play the Elf on the Shelf game?

This small book is about protecting the truth of the birth of Christ as we celebrate Christmas each year, though we should remember that we celebrate Christmas each and every Sunday as we worship Christ and give thanks for His birth, life, death, resurrection, and ascension. Every Sunday is Christmas! But if the dangers of commercialism, sentimentalism, and syncretism lurk about our Christmas celebrations each year, what can we do to ensure that we do not distort, dilute, or diminish the truths surrounding Christ's birth? The simplest answer is to meditate upon the scriptural accounts of Christ's birth—examine every detail so we can insulate our hearts from the world's efforts to silence the gospel, as well as from our own tendencies to forget the reason for the season.

The first chapter on Mary's Magnificat examines Mary's song of praise and observes how familiar she was with the

Old Testament. She was well versed with God's covenant promises, and thus her song is filled with numerous rich Old Testament allusions. When the angel announced that Mary would give birth to the Messiah, she had a biblical frame of reference both to understand the message and to fill her heart with praise. Her song revels in God's faithfulness throughout the ages. At Christmas, do we join with Mary and celebrate God's fidelity to His promises and people in giving us Jesus, the Messiah?

Chapter 2 reflects upon Luke's narrative about Christ's birth and the angelic announcement to the shepherds who were tending their flocks by night. This fantastic announcement is the frequent topic of Christmas hymns and sacred art, but key details in the event and birth proclamation often get left behind. The presence of angels signals titanic events in redemptive history—the unfolding of redemption and judgment. The angels also announced that the Savior would bring peace upon those with whom God was pleased, not peace on earth and goodwill to all men, as in some Christmas hymns. Christ's birth announcement is about God's sovereign gift of salvation and faith in the gospel of Christ. At Christmas, do we join the shepherds and worship Jesus, the King of Kings and Lord of Lords?

Chapter 3 explores a well-known Christmas hymn, "O Come, O Come, Emmanuel," which was written in the Middle Ages. One of the best ways to ensure that we are not swept away by our culture's misguided beliefs is to look back to the past to see how our ancestors celebrated Christ's birth. The Middle Ages did not struggle with commercialism, for example, so it is instructive to see what thoughts occupied the hearts and minds of Christians during this period. The ancient hymn rehearses many great Old Testament themes, notably the promise of the Davidic heir and the Egyptian and Babylonian exoduses. Medieval Christians saw their condition as living in exile from the presence of God and thus longed for the advent of Christ. The first advent was a harbinger of hope for Christ's second advent. When we sing Christmas hymns, do they give us rich, deep, and lasting truths about Christ's birth, or are they trite jingles that dilute the gospel? Do we tap into the devotion of our ancestors to help keep us focused upon Christ during the Christmas holidays?

Chapter 4 examines another popular subject of Christmas music and art—the visit of the wise men. The fact that the wise men brought Jesus gifts is an oft-cited reason for why we give gifts at Christmas. But a number of details from the narrative should make us stop, sit up, and ask some questions: Why were gentiles coming to worship Jesus when His own people were fearful of His birth and even sought to murder Him? And while the wise men did present gifts, they did not give gifts to one another but to Jesus. We can certainly give gifts to one another at Christmas, but does Christmas remind us that we need to give gifts, chiefly above everyone else, to our triune God? Do we offer God the gifts of sacrifice, praise, and worship? Do the wise men remind us that, as gentiles, we do not belong but have nevertheless been drawn nigh by God's grace in Christ?

The fifth and final chapter looks at the Nunc Dimittis ("Now you are letting"), which are the opening words from the Latin Bible of Simeon's prayer of thanksgiving upon beholding the infant Savior. All too often people consciously or unconsciously pit the Old Testament against the New: God was angry in the Old, surrounded by ominous clouds, fire, and lightning, whereas Jesus appears humble, meek, and lowly as an infant. The so-called god of the Old Testament was one of wrath, and the so-called god of the New Testament is one of love. As common as these thoughts might be, Simeon's prayer reminds us that God is the same yesterday, today, and tomorrow. The birth of Christ is ultimately unintelligible apart from God's self-revelation in the Old Testament. The fact that Simeon encounters God incarnate in the temple *outside the holy of holies* informs us that the infant Savior comes wrapped in the swaddling cloths of Old Testament revelation. The irrefutable connections between the Old and New Testaments explain why Simeon was so joyful at beholding the Messiah. When we meditate upon the birth of Christ, do we see this event as the culmination of many Old Testament promises, once again revealing God's faithfulness throughout the ages?

In the end, this book is not about robbing us of the joy of Christmas but rather refocusing our delight upon Christ—the reason for the season. This wee book aims to take Christ out of the cradle of culture and return Him to the manger of Scripture. My chief goal is to ensure that when we celebrate the birth of Christ, the light of the gospel is what shines brightest in our hearts, and commercialism, sentimentalism, and syncretism never cast a shadow upon God's mercy in Christ.

---✽---

MARY'S MAGNIFICAT

My soul magnifies the Lord,
And my spirit has rejoiced in God my Savior.
For He has regarded the lowly state of His maidservant;
For behold, henceforth all generations will call me blessed.
For He who is mighty has done great things for me,
And holy is His name.
And His mercy is on those who fear Him
From generation to generation.
He has shown strength with His arm;
He has scattered the proud in the imagination of their hearts.
He has put down the mighty from their thrones,
And exalted the lowly.
He has filled the hungry with good things,
And the rich He has sent away empty.
He has helped His servant Israel,
In remembrance of His mercy,
As He spoke to our fathers,
To Abraham and to his seed forever.

—Luke 1:46–55

---✽---

1

Mary's Magnificat

Each year, Christmas displays are put up in stores, lights and decorations adorn homes, and illuminated Santas, snowmen, reindeer, and nativity scenes magically appear on lawns across the nation. As familiar as we are with the themes of Christmas, the culture at large does not truly understand the reason for the season. In the flurry of holiday cheer, even Christians who want to celebrate the birth of Christ might lose track of the real Christmas story. We know the basic outline of Christ's birth narrative: the angel announces to Mary that she will give birth to a son, the Messiah, and then we fast forward to the angelic host and the infant child as He lies in the manger. Our minds likely drift to Christmas carols:

> Angels we have heard on high
> Sweetly singing o'er the plains
> And the mountains in reply
> Echoing their joyous strains

Yet I wonder how often we stop to ponder Mary's response to Gabriel's announcement that she would miraculously give birth to a child, let alone the Messiah. Have you ever paused and reflected upon her song of praise, what the church has historically called the Magnificat? Have you considered her words in light of the Old Testament, or as a model expression of faith in the gospel? These are important questions that we want to ask of Mary's song of praise, her prayer, so that we can ensure that we do not lose track of the true meaning of Christmas.

Mary's Knowledge of the Old Testament

Mary's song of responsive praise is one of the few New Testament psalms. In fact, the original church order produced by the Synod of Dort (1618–19) authorized, among other passages, the 150 psalms of David, the Ten Commandments, and Mary's Magnificat as suitable for use in worship for congregational singing. The pastors and theologians at the synod believed that Mary's Magnificat was equivalent to a psalm and thus worthy of use in corporate worship. This means that Mary's song is nothing like many of the cotton-candy jingles often associated with Christmas, such as "Frosty the Snowman" or "Rudolph the Red-Nosed Reindeer." These jingles are indelibly inscribed on our collective psyche, but they have no substance. This is certainly not the case with Mary's song. We cannot explore every single Old Testament allusion and reference in Mary's song, as this would exceed the modest scope of this brief chapter. Nevertheless, we can look at one example.

On the heels of receiving Gabriel's announcement, Mary responds:

> My soul magnifies the Lord,
> And my spirit has rejoiced in God my Savior.
> For He has regarded the lowly state of His
>   maidservant;
> For behold, henceforth all generations will call me
>   blessed. (Luke:1:46–47)

Mary does not compose her words from scratch but instead borrows (under inspiration of the Spirit) from the Old Testament. Her words are reminiscent of the psalmist's:

> I will bless the LORD at all times;
> His praise shall continually be in my mouth.
> My soul shall make its boast in the LORD;
> The humble shall hear of it and be glad.
> Oh, magnify the LORD with me,
> And let us exalt His name together. (Ps. 34:1–3)

Mary also echoes Hannah, another young woman who was blessed with the miraculous birth of a son:

> My heart rejoices in the LORD;
> My horn is exalted in the LORD.
> I smile at my enemies,
> Because I rejoice in Your salvation. (1 Sam. 2:1)

There are striking parallels between Mary's song and these two Old Testament passages, which means that she regularly fed upon the Word of God, so much so that when she expressed her joy and praise, scriptural thoughts and themes flowed forth from her heart. Prick Mary's finger and Scripture ran out. At the same time, I think Mary was acutely aware of the momentous nature of Gabriel's announcement, which is why she echoes the words of Hannah. Hannah was one of a number of women in biblical history who were blessed with the special promised birth of children, including Hagar (Gen. 16:11), Sarah (18:10, 14), and Manoah's wife, who gave birth to Samson (Judges 13). When Mary, therefore, echoes Hannah's words of praise, she implicitly acknowledges that an earth-shattering event is underway. Mary was undoubtedly surprised by both the angel's presence and announcement, but her deep knowledge of Scripture immediately helped her to know where she fit in the big picture of God's unfolding plan of redemption.

Mary's intimate knowledge of the Old Testament should cause us to ask how well we know our Bibles. Bible illiteracy is at an all-time high. In past generations, seminaries could count on new students to come to study for the ministry with a solid grasp of Scripture, whether because they were raised in the church, catechized in doctrine, or encouraged to memorize Scripture. Theological institutions can no longer make this assumption, and some schools have added basic Bible courses to their curricula to address the problem. But Bible knowledge is not only for future pastors but for every Christian. Children learn to speak by repeating their parents' words back to them. We can apply the same principle to the children of God. We learn to speak words of praise by repeating God's own Word back to Him. Do we know enough Scripture to speak biblically shaped words of praise back to our heavenly Father?

Mary's Praise

One of the benefits of using God's Word in songs of praise, in prayers, and in conversation with others about God is that they remind us of who God is and who we are. The Word of God is a map to the cosmos that helps us to see the grandeur and immensity of the creation and our Creator and, conversely, our infinitesimal place within this vast universe. As Mary uttered her Old Testament-infused words of praise, she was overcome with a sense of her unworthiness and God's grace: "For He has regarded the lowly state of His maidservant" (Luke 1:48). She surveyed the landscape of redemptive history and saw God's faithfulness and His promises landing on her: "For He who is mighty has done great things for me, and holy is His name" (v. 49). She likely recalled the severity of God's just judgments against His enemies, such as Pharaoh and his army, King Ahab and Queen Jezebel, and Nebuchadnezzar, who was humbled to roam on all fours like a beast: "He has put down the mighty from their thrones, and exalted the lowly" (v. 52). She was also familiar with the meek and lowly people He cared for through His providence, like Ruth and Naomi: "He has filled the hungry with good things, and the rich He has sent away empty" (v. 53).

Given Mary's knowledge of redemptive history, that God humbled the proud and mighty and exalted the lowly, she knew that God's mercy did not fall indiscriminately upon all but only on His covenant people. In her song she says, "He has shown strength with His arm; He has scattered the proud in the imagination of their hearts" (v. 51). This statement has roots that go back to Exodus: "I am the LORD; I will bring you out from under the burdens of the Egyptians, I will rescue you from their bondage, and I will redeem you with an outstretched arm and with great judgments" (Ex. 6:6). Note that Mary's song uses the same imagery—the arm of God.

God, however, did not outstretch His arm to redeem the nations but only His people, Israel. Mary knew that God gave promises to Adam and Eve (Gen. 3:15), to Abraham (as we will see below), and to King David (2 Sam.

7:14–16). Praise filled her heart because she saw the scarlet thread of God's love running from our first parents, through Israel and King David, and coming to her. As she beheld the sky of God's sovereignty studded with so many brilliant stars of His mercy and grace, she was overwhelmed that God now rested and shone the light of the star of His promised Messiah over her. In the vast cosmos of God's love, she saw her insignificance and reveled in the gift of His grace. Do we likewise stop amid the flurry of the busy Christmas season and reflect upon the fact that the scarlet cord of God's love in Christ that stretches all the way back to Adam and Eve has come to us? Do words of thanksgiving and praise for our triune God flow from our hearts?

Mary's Faith

One of the most important points in Mary's song is her faith, which stands out in the broader context of this passage. The frame of her song is crucial for a proper appreciation of its significance. In the overall literary and narrative course of his gospel, Luke purposefully sets Mary's response in contrast to Zacharias's reaction. Zacharias was "righteous before God, walking in all the commandments and ordinances of the Lord blameless" (Luke 1:6). An angel appeared to him and announced the birth of his son, John (vv. 11–17). Zacharias's initial response was disbelief, and so the angel silenced him (vv. 18–20). When the angel, however, came to Mary, her response was very different. She asked the angel how she would give birth, not out of doubt, but from a place of wonder because she was a virgin (v. 34). Nevertheless, her answer was filled with faith in the word of God that came through the angel: "Behold the maidservant of the Lord! Let it be to me according to your word" (v. 38).

Mary's faith-filled, gospel-centered, Christ-exalting reply clearly emerges in the concluding words of her song:

> He has helped His servant Israel,
> In remembrance of His mercy,
> As He spoke to our fathers,
> To Abraham and to his seed forever. (vv. 54–55)

Mary specifically looked to and knew of God's promise to Abraham—the promise that God would give him an heir, a promise that Paul calls the gospel: "And the Scripture, foreseeing that God would justify the Gentiles by faith, preached the gospel to Abraham beforehand, saying, 'In you all the nations shall be blessed.' So then those who are of faith are blessed with believing Abraham" (Gal. 3:8–9). Mary was blessed along with Abraham because she possessed faith in the promised Messiah. She responded in faith to the angel's announcement, and she looked by faith to God's gospel promise to Abraham. Mary ultimately looked by faith to her Son, who would redeem the people of God from their sin.

The announcement of Christ's birth is the long-awaited fulfillment of God's promises to His people, a promise He first made to Adam and Eve on the heels of their act of covenantal treason:

> And I will put enmity
> Between you and the woman,
> And between your seed and her Seed;

He shall bruise your head,
And you shall bruise His heel. (Gen. 3:15)

Zacharias and Mary both believed in the promise because God gave them the free gift of faith by His grace, but Zacharias initially clouded his faith with doubt. Such doubt can rob us of peace. The Westminster Confession of Faith (WCF), for example, says, "True believers may have the assurance of their salvation divers ways shaken, diminished, and intermitted…yet are they never so utterly destitute of that seed of God, and life of faith, that love of Christ and the brethren, that sincerity of heart, and conscience of duty, out of which, by the operation of the Spirit, this assurance may, in due time, be revived" (18.4).

What Mary's song should remind us, then, is that God is faithful to His promises. As Paul writes, "For all the promises of God in [Christ] are Yes, and in Him Amen" (2 Cor. 1:20). As much of a blessing as the Christmas season can be—that yearly reminder of God's fulfillment of His promises through the birth of His Son—we should not forget that we celebrate the birth of Christ every Lord's Day. Every time we gather for corporate worship on Sunday, we collectively praise God for sending His Son—for His incarnation, His life of perfect obedience, His suffering and death on the cross, His resurrection from the dead, and His present intercession on our behalf as He reigns in royal session at the Father's right hand. While we may have doubts like Zacharias, we should pray that God would fill our hearts with the faith of Mary, a faith that looked to the promised Messiah with hope that God would save His people from their sins through His only begotten Son.

Conclusion

When Mary received Gabriel's announcement that she would give birth to the Messiah, God blessed her by His grace through the sovereign work of the Spirit so that she would have faith in the gospel. She was also, however, well prepared for this announcement because she possessed an intimate knowledge of the Old Testament. God had laid a foundation for the announcement of His Son's birth in Mary by writing His word upon the walls of her heart. When she heard the announcement, therefore, she was filled with praise because she knew God was faithful to His promises and that she, lowly as she was, was the recipient of God's grace in Christ. Each year as we celebrate Christmas and each Sunday that we gather to worship our triune God, we should pray for grace that we too would receive the message of the gospel with faith, thanksgiving, and praise—that we would write Mary's song upon the walls of our hearts. We must not let the "spirit of the season" draw our faith away from God's faithfulness to His promises, our sinfulness and unworthiness, and God's gospel grace in Christ. If we find our hearts drifting away in the currents of holiday cheer, we would do well to anchor our souls upon Mary's Magnificat and take her words of praise upon our lips.

Questions for Reflection

1. Can you identify passages of Scripture in the Old Testament that prophesy of the birth of the Messiah other than those mentioned above?

2. What psalms might you draw upon to highlight your own unworthiness and, conversely, God's great mercy in salvation?

3. Why should we celebrate the birth of Christ every Lord's Day?

4. If we are stricken with doubts about God's love, to what passages of Scripture might we turn? How does His faithfulness throughout the ages help weaken our doubts?

---✻---

THE BIRTH OF CHRIST

Now there were in the same country shepherds living out in the fields, keeping watch over their flock by night. And behold, an angel of the Lord stood before them, and the glory of the Lord shone around them, and they were greatly afraid. Then the angel said to them, "Do not be afraid, for behold, I bring you good tidings of great joy which will be to all people. For there is born to you this day in the city of David a Savior, who is Christ the Lord. And this will be the sign to you: You will find a Babe wrapped in swaddling cloths, lying in a manger."

And suddenly there was with the angel a multitude of the heavenly host praising God and saying:

"Glory to God in the highest,
And on earth peace, goodwill toward men!"

So it was, when the angels had gone away from them into heaven, that the shepherds said to one another, "Let us now go to Bethlehem and see this thing that has come to pass, which the Lord has made known to us." And they came with haste and found Mary and Joseph, and the Babe lying in a manger. Now when they had seen Him, they made widely known the saying which was told them concerning this Child. And all those who heard it marveled at those things which were told them by the shepherds. But Mary kept all these things and pondered them in her heart. Then the shepherds returned, glorifying and praising God for all the things that they had heard and seen, as it was told them.

—Luke 2:8–20

---✻---

2

The Birth of Christ

Christ's birth is a theological truth that has now become a cultural image. Snatched from the manger of Scripture, the infant Christ has been placed into the cultural cradle of icons. For example, a colleague of mine was once walking by the window of a downtown Tokyo department store during Christmas when he spied the seasonal display: the baby Jesus in His manger surrounded by the seven dwarves. The world has taken Jesus and embraced Him because they like the miracle child who brings tidings of peace, not necessarily the Messiah who heralds the gospel, a message that requires sinners to repent.

If we look more closely at Christ's birth account and return Jesus to the manger of Scripture, the fact that angels attend His birth should signal that we behold something holy, unique, and earth-shattering. Our culture, however, with some unfortunate help from the church, has also swept angels into the cultural cradle of icons. The church has historically portrayed angels as chubby babies with wings, which is a deflection from Scripture. Following this trend, our culture regularly portrays angels in movies, books, and television shows and even uses them for mascots and names of sports teams, which are all too human. Yet, if we closely examine what the Bible has to say about angels, we will find some much-needed light cast upon the birth of Christ. We can quietly and politely remove Christ from the cultural cradle and return Him to the manger of Scripture.

Angels

What does the Bible have to say about angels? The term *angel* is a transliteration of the Greek term *angelos*, and is the translation of the Hebrew Old Testament term *malach*, which means "messenger." In fact, the Old Testament prophet's name *Malachi* means "My messenger." If we pause and disassociate the term *angel* from our common understanding—either fat babies with wings or attractive women with wings—and return to the Bible's messenger concept, a very different picture emerges.

As we survey various Old Testament passages, we see that angels often wielded messages of judgment. They heralded the destruction of Sodom (Genesis 19); led the Israelites through the wilderness, bringing judgment on those who did not obey (Ex. 23:20–21); and struck down 185,000 Assyrians (Isa. 37:36). The psalmist speaks of companies of destroying angels (Ps. 78:49). In the book of Revelation, angels announce the seven trumpets of judgment against the unbelieving world and pour out the bowls of God's wrath upon the earth (chapters 8–11, 16).

When angels have personally appeared to saints throughout redemptive history, they have struck fear and awe in those who beheld them. When Balaam encountered the angel of the Lord with his sword drawn in his hand, he immediately bowed down and fell on his face in his presence (Num. 22:31). When an angel appeared to the apostle

John, he too fell on his face to worship him until the angel forbade him from doing this (Rev. 19:10). Angels are fearsome creatures, and this explains why the shepherds were fearful when the host of angels first appeared to them: "And behold, an angel of the Lord stood before them, and the glory of the Lord shone around them, and they were greatly afraid" (Luke 2:9). Had this been a company of fat, winged infants, I very much doubt that fear would have gripped the shepherds.

If the shepherds had even the slightest knowledge of the Old Testament, they would have dreaded the angels because they would have thought that they had appeared to bring judgment, as they had done against Sodom or Egypt. But angels do not merely presage judgment; they also appear when there are major tectonic shifts in redemptive history.

Another factor should alert us that something unique is afoot. In previous angelic appearances, we typically see angels in small numbers of one to three. But in this case an entire angelic host bursts onto the scene to make their announcement. This massive company of angels should signal to us that something unique is about to occur. If we see Jesus in His native, scriptural setting rather than in our culture—surrounded by the heavenly host rather than the seven dwarves—we allow Scripture rather than culture to shape our understanding of Christ's birth.

Angels are not tame, adorable creatures but are agents of divine revelation, heralds of judgment and salvation. They are the stewards and revealers of God's plan of redemption, a message that focuses upon the gospel of

Christ. The presence of angels should immediately signal that we stand on holy ground in the presence of God, something that should fill us with awe and praise, not merely sentimentalism or commercialism.

Their Message
In spite of the great fear that the angels instilled in the shepherds, they did not appear to bring a message of judgment but one of hope, joy, and salvation: "Do not be afraid, for behold, I bring you good tidings of great joy which will be to all people. For there is born to you this day in the city of David a Savior, who is Christ the Lord" (Luke 2:10–11). Far from a message of judgment, the angel's words were filled with hope. The angel's message, heralding the birth of the Messiah, was a train pulling a number of Old Testament cars chock-full of significance and meaning. Faithful Israelites would have been intimately familiar with the idea of the messiah from passages such as Psalm 2:

> Why do the nations rage,
> And the people plot a vain thing?
> The kings of the earth set themselves,
> And the rulers take counsel together,
> Against the Lord and against His Anointed
>   [messiah]. (vv. 1–2)

The Messiah would deliver Israel and subdue the nations and restore God's reign throughout the world. The angel also says that the Messiah was born in the city of David, which confirmed His royal lineage and placed God's faithfulness to His covenant promises on full display. God promised David that He would seat one of his descendants on the throne to reign eternally over Israel (2 Sam. 7:16).

But the angel's announcement also reveals a number of seemingly inherent tensions bound with Christ's ministry. On the one hand, no earthly king ever received a regal, angelic birth announcement like Jesus—God rent the heavens open, and a myriad of angels proceeded forth to announce to the world that the long-awaited Messiah, the King of Kings and Lord of Lords, had been born. On the other hand, there are clues revealing that this King's reign would be different from all others. Jesus was born and wrapped in swaddling cloths, not the garments of royalty. The infant king was not placed in a plush royal cradle but in an animal feeding trough (Luke 2:12). The angels did not make their announcement in the halls of power to kings and princes, but to the lowest of the low, to shepherds.

People in the first-century world looked upon shepherds as thieves because they often allowed their flocks to graze on other people's property. The culture despised shepherds because they worked far from home and were therefore unable to protect their families or defend their homes. Plus, the simple truth of the matter is, if you spend time with animals, you will end up smelling like one. Although the event was removed by some fifteen hundred years, Joseph told his brothers that "every shepherd is an abomination to the Egyptians" (Gen. 46:34). These facts highlight the great heights from which the Son of God condescended and entered into the fallen, sinful human condition—He was God in the flesh but nevertheless came under a veil of humility. But to what end did He come?

The angel announced, "Glory to God in the highest, and on earth peace among those with whom he is pleased!" (Luke 2:14 ESV). Here I cite the English Standard Version because, in my own opinion (though I am aware that others will disagree with me), it sharpens the translation of the underlying Greek. The angels brought a message of peace—but this is not the peace that many associate with the Christmas season. The culture has taken this message and garbled the text. In a well-known Christmas song "I Heard the Bells on Christmas Day," singers such as Harry Belafonte, Bing Crosby, and Johnny Cash have crooned:

> I heard the bells on Christmas day
> Their old familiar carols play,
> And wild and sweet the words repeat
> Of peace on earth, goodwill to men.

"Peace on earth, goodwill to men" has been etched into our collective mind. The same misrepresentation appears in another Christmas favorite, "The Gloria," which states: "Glory to God in the highest, and on earth peace to people of goodwill."

This is *not* what the angel said. The angel specifically said that God's peace would fall upon those "with whom he is pleased" (Luke 2:14 ESV). The promised peace is not "world peace"—the constant pursuit of activists, politicians, and college students—but the sovereign electing favor of God. The faithful Israelites had longed for peace, a peace that came from beholding the face of God: "The LORD bless you and keep you; the LORD make His face shine upon you, and be gracious to you; the LORD lift up His countenance upon you, and give you *peace*" (Num. 6:24–27, emphasis added). On the heels of murdering his brother, Cain feared not being allowed to behold the face of God: "Surely You have driven me out this day from the face of the ground; I shall be hidden from Your face" (Gen. 4:14).

God's peace, however, comes through only one person, as Paul writes: "Therefore, having been justified by faith, we have peace with God through our Lord Jesus Christ" (Rom. 5:1). On our own, we are sinners who rightly deserve God's just condemnation, and the only way to escape this judgment is through Christ. God, however, decides upon whom His favor falls. Not only does the angel's announcement say this—"on earth peace among those with whom he is pleased"—but the very announcement itself embodies the message. God did not make the announcement to all of Israel but specifically showed His favor to lowly shepherds.

The Shepherds' Response

How did the shepherds respond? "They came with haste and found Mary and Joseph, and the Babe lying in a manger" (Luke 2:16). The shepherds did not hesitate for a moment but immediately rushed off to look for the newborn King. They did not go to gawk, stare, or marvel but went to worship: "Then the shepherds returned, glorifying and praising God for all the things that they had heard and seen, as it was told them" (v. 20). They praised God because they had beheld the Messiah for themselves, and they now wanted to share with others the awe-inspiring message proclaimed by an angelic host: "There is born to you this day…a Savior, who is Christ the Lord" (v. 11). Their response was not only amazement but thankfulness for God's faithfulness. They longed for the fulfillment of God's promises—His promise to Adam and Eve to deliver them through the Seed of the woman (Gen. 3:15), His promise to give Abraham an heir from his very own body through whom every nation would be blessed (15:1–5; 22:18), His continued promises to Isaac and Jacob (Ps. 105:5–8), His promises to Judah that the scepter would not depart from between his feet until the Messiah would claim it (Gen. 49:8–10), the promises to David that one of his sons would rule over Israel forever (2 Sam. 7:14–16)—and so they rejoiced in God's faithfulness.

The shepherds likely did not know how the infant King would save them, but at least for that moment, on that night of nights, they had peace because they beheld the face of God in the face of Jesus, the Christ. They did not know that nails would one day pierce the infant's tiny hands; that a crown of thorns would be thrust upon His small brow; that His little ears would have contempt, blasphemy, ridicule, and hate poured into them; or that His diminutive eyes would look down from the cross through drops of sweat and blood as He beheld the people gathering at His feet to mock and deride Him. What they did know was that they beheld the Messiah, and they rightly praised and worshiped God for the privilege of being the first to receive the glorious news.

Conclusion

As we visit the manger and behold the newborn Christ through the eyes of faith, we must pay careful attention to God's Word. We may fear that if we look too closely at the birth of Christ that we will lose cherished ideas, emotions, and joys that we associate with the Christmas season. While we may have to surrender the popular message of Christmas—peace on earth and goodwill to men announced by chubby babies with wings—what we gain in return is far greater. We surrender a message of sentimentality, where the seven dwarves stand guard over the infant Messiah.

In its place we receive a message of God's faithfulness and hope, a message that God has come into the world to save sinners, and He has done so through the incarnation of His Son, Jesus, through whom we have peace with God. Through the sovereign gift of faith, we can rest under the mighty wings of Christ, the wings that shelter us from God's just wrath, and we know eternal peace as we behold the face of God in the face of Jesus. This is a message that should cause us, like the shepherds, to glorify and praise God for all we have heard and seen, as it has been told to us through the Bible's account of Christ's birth.

Questions for Reflection

1. In what ways are we like the shepherds
   (hint: 1 Cor. 1:26–29)?

2. How does the angelic announcement highlight
   that God's saving grace does not fall universally
   upon all people?

3. How does Christ's birth begin to show the truth
   of Paul's words, that Jesus "made Himself of no
   reputation, taking the form of a bondservant"
   (Phil. 2:7)?

4. What is significant about the fact that angels
   announced the birth of the Messiah?

✳

O COME, O COME, EMMANUEL

O come, O come, Emmanuel,
And ransom captive Israel,
That mourns in lonely exile here,
Until the Son of God appear.

Rejoice! Rejoice! Emmanuel
Shall come to thee, O Israel.

O come, O come, Thou Lord of might,
Who to Thy tribes, on Sinai's height,
In ancient times didst give the law
In cloud and majesty and awe.

Rejoice! Rejoice! Emmanuel
Shall come to thee, O Israel.

O come, Thou Rod of Jesse, free
Thine own from Satan's tyranny;
From depths of hell Thy people save,
And give them victory o'er the grave.

Rejoice! Rejoice! Emmanuel
Shall come to thee, O Israel.

O come, Thou Dayspring from on high,
And cheer us by Thy drawing nigh;
Disperse the gloomy clouds of night,
And death's dark shadows put to flight.

Rejoice! Rejoice! Emmanuel
Shall come to thee, O Israel.

O come, Thou Key of David, come
And open wide our heavenly home;
Make safe the way that leads on high,
And close the path to misery.

Rejoice! Rejoice! Emmanuel
Shall come to thee, O Israel.

———————————✳———————————

3

O Come, O Come, Emmanuel

"O Come, O Come, Emmanuel" is one of the better-known hymns typically sung during the Christmas season. It originated in the Middle Ages, around AD 800, as an antiphon, or anthem. It was then restructured into verse form in the 1100s and was eventually published in a Latin hymnal in 1710. The hymn was later discovered, translated, and published in 1851 by John Mason Neale, an Anglican minister. As people sing this hymn, they assuredly know that they are singing about the birth of Christ.

However, what is striking about this hymn is its approach to unpacking the birth of Christ. It moves from the shadowlands of the Old Testament into the light of the New Testament with the revelation of God in Christ. This hymn traces the experience of exile and exodus throughout God's redemptive plan, from Israel's captivity in Babylon to our eschatological, or final, exodus that began with the birth of the Messiah.

One of the best things we can do when we celebrate Christmas is to join hands with the church throughout the ages to see what we can learn from our ancestors. We can let the fresh breeze of the centuries blow through our hearts and minds to teach us how to rejoice in the birth of Christ in deeper, richer, and more meaningful ways—ways that are not shaped by our culture's commercialism.

Mourning in Lonely Exile

In Israel's earliest days, God brought them out of Egypt, made a covenant with them, and began to lead them to the land of promise—the land that He had sworn to give to Abraham and his descendants (Gen. 15:18–21). Israel, of course, was a cantankerous nation and lacked the faith to enter the promised land, to believe in the gospel promise of God (Heb. 3:18–4:2).

When Israel finished their forty-year wandering and stood at the threshold of the promised land, it was undoubtedly a time of excitement and hope. They were at last going to enter the land promised to their patriarch Abraham so long ago. On the eve of their entry into the land, Moses wrote an inspired prophetic song. This song was filled with praises for their covenant Lord, but at the same time foretold of Israel's future disobedience and sin (Deut. 32:20–24). Israel sadly fulfilled these words and was carried into exile because of their sin, idolatry, and rebellion. The Northern Kingdom was taken away by the Assyrians in the eighth century BC, and the Southern Kingdom of Judah was taken into captivity by the Babylonians in the sixth century BC.

Over the centuries there have been millions of people displaced by war—exiled from their home countries. Yet Israel's exile in Babylon was unique. Israel was the only nation on the face of the earth with whom God had made a covenant. God gave Israel, His firstborn son (Ex. 4:22), a fruitful land flowing with milk and honey, a land marked by God's very own presence as in the garden-temple of Eden. In the same way that God once walked with

Adam—also His firstborn son (Luke 3:38)—in the beautiful garden-temple (Gen. 3:8), so too God walked with Israel in the promised land by His presence in the tabernacle (Lev. 26:11–12; 2 Sam. 7:6). Yet, like Adam before them, Israel sinned and broke God's covenant.

Again like Adam, Israel was exiled from the presence of God. They were banished to Babylon, longing for God's presence, longing for God to redeem them, to ransom them from their captivity. However, the faithful remnant did not desire merely to return to the land but ultimately for God to dwell once again in their midst (Ps. 137:1–4). Yet, as Israel sat in exile by the waters of Babylon, there was still hope—a hope of redemption. Many undoubtedly looked to the prophetic words of Isaiah: "Behold, the virgin shall conceive and bear a Son, and shall call His name Immanuel" (Isa. 7:14). There was a coming child, One who would save Israel—the Lord's presence in the flesh. In this regard we should note that the word *Immanuel*, or *Emmanuel*, means, "God with us."

Perhaps now we have a better idea of what lies behind the first two verses of this hymn:

> O come, O come, Emmanuel,
> And ransom captive Israel,
> That mourns in lonely exile here,
> Until the Son of God appear.
> Rejoice! Rejoice! Emmanuel
> Shall come to thee, O Israel.
>
> O come, O come, Thou Lord of might,
> Who to Thy tribes, on Sinai's height,

> In ancient times didst give the law
> In cloud and majesty and awe.

In these verses the hymn recounts the faithful remnant in exile in Babylon, longing and looking for the birth of their Savior. This desire is couched in terms of the biblical theme of the eschatological exodus, evident in the connection between Israel's exile in Babylon and the exodus from Egypt by reference to God's presence on Sinai.

The Shoot of Jesse and Key of David

The prophet Isaiah, however, had much more to say about this coming Savior. Many Old Testament saints knew that the coming Savior would be from the line of David (2 Sam. 7:12–13). However, the nation would be in ruin, the temple—God's dwelling place—would be razed to a pile of rubble, and it would seem as though David's line was cut off. Once again, Isaiah prophesied, "There shall come forth a Rod from the stem of Jesse, and a Branch shall grow out of his roots" (Isa. 11:1). Isaiah likens the Davidic dynasty to a stump—the great oak of David's kingdom that once vaulted into the heavens was cut to the ground and seemingly all but destroyed. Yet, from this stump a shoot would go forth—and this shoot would bear much fruit. Unlike Israel's wicked kings, even unlike King David, this future King would be personally, perpetually, and perfectly holy and righteous (vv. 2–5).

Elsewhere in Isaiah's prophecies, there was an oracle of judgment against Jerusalem and especially her king, who relied too much on other nations rather than on the Lord. Isaiah prophesied that God would raise an insignificant servant to care for the house of David, Eliakim, the son of Hilkiah:

> The key of the house of David
> I will lay on his shoulder;
> So he shall open, and no one shall shut;
> And he shall shut, and no one shall open.
>   (Isa. 22:22)

Yet Eliakim pointed forward to the greater Servant, to the One who would possess the key of the house of David. We read in the book of Revelation:

> And to the angel of the church in Philadelphia write,
>
> "These things says He who is holy, He who is true, 'He who has the key of David, He who opens and no one shuts, and shuts and no one opens.'" (3:7)

The apostle John applies this Isaian title to Jesus. Jesus is the one, of course—the Son of David, the Son of God—who would come and rule Israel. Faithful Israelites undoubtedly longed and looked for the birth of this child, the One who would hold the key of David. This Isaian theme of the Davidic key appears in the fifth verse of the hymn:

> O come, Thou Key of David, come
> And open wide our heavenly home;
> Make safe the way that leads on high,
> And close the path to misery.

Notice once again the theme of the exodus, as it is the Davidic descendant who will make safe the way that leads on high—the pilgrimage to the New Jerusalem, the fulfillment of the shadow of the promised land.

Dayspring from on High

Though hundreds of years passed from Isaiah's day, seemingly little had happened to address Israel's exilic mourning. Yes, Israel had returned from exile—Cyrus, the Persian king, led Israel back to the land and permitted them to rebuild the temple (Isaiah 45; Ezra 1). Israel left Babylon on an exodus-like journey that returned them to the land of their forefathers (Isa. 42:16; 48:21; 49:10; Ex. 13:21–22; 15:13, respectively).

Yet, even though the temple had been rebuilt, the faithful remnant knew that their return to the land was not the great divine visitation for which they longed, hoped, and prayed. In fact, when the temple was rebuilt, Israel wept rather than rejoiced. The prophet Haggai lamented: "Who is left among you who saw this temple in its former glory? And how do you see it now? In comparison with it, is this not in your eyes as nothing?" (Hag. 2:3). But Haggai's sight was not exhausted by the lackluster temple that stood before him; he looked to the horizon with hope: "'The glory of this latter temple shall be greater than the former,' says the LORD of hosts. 'And in this place I will give peace,' says the LORD of hosts" (v. 9). So, then, Israel was still looking for a greater day, one that looked beyond this provisional return to the land. That day would come hundreds of years later.

On the heels of the birth of John the Baptist, John's father, Zacharias, prophesied of the Messiah who would soon appear (Luke 1:67–79). Zacharias likens the coming Messiah—the descendant of David, the One who would deliver Israel from her enemies, who would be righteous, who would bring the forgiveness of sins and light to those who sat in darkness—to the sunrise, or Dayspring, from on high (v. 78). In other words, he likens the coming Messiah to the rising sun shining light upon the dark world (see also John 1:1–5). The birth of the Savior was the means by which God would liberate His people from the powers of Satan, sin, and death. And, hence, we find the following in the fourth verse of the hymn:

> O come, Thou Dayspring from on high,
> And cheer us by Thy drawing nigh;
> Disperse the gloomy clouds of night,
> And death's dark shadows put to flight.

God with Us

Emmanuel, God with us, did come to Israel. God fulfilled His promises that He made long ago, not just through the prophet Isaiah but even to our very first parents, Adam and Eve. God promised Adam and Eve that the Seed of the woman would overcome the seed of the serpent (Gen. 3:15). Ever since then, God's faithful had been looking for the birth of their Savior. When Jesus was born, God finally answered the prayers of His people. He had finally fulfilled His long-awaited promise (see Luke 2:4–14). Here was the son of David, the Lord, the One who would deliver His people from their sin.

Christ was not born to bring political freedom to the people of God but a freedom of far greater significance. He was to bring freedom from the powers of Satan, sin, and death. Given what appears in the first two verses, the third verse of the hymn casts Christ's redemption in terms of the eschatological, or final, exodus. The exodus is deliverance neither from Pharaoh's tyranny nor from Babylon. Rather, we behold the exodus out from under the oppressive rule of Satan, sin, and death that only Jesus brings:

> O come, Thou Rod of Jesse, free
> Thine own from Satan's tyranny;
> From depths of hell Thy people save,
> And give them victory o'er the grave.

The writers of this ancient hymn knew that the earlier Egyptian and Babylonian exoduses were pointing forward to the last great and final exodus that One greater than Moses and Cyrus would launch. They contemplated this redemptive pattern as they celebrated Christmas.

Conclusion

When we meditate on Christ's birth, we must not do so in terms of some sort of sugar-coated tale about an infant king born to bring the world some joy, to give some glimmer of hope in an otherwise gloomy place. When we think of the birth of Christ we should also not get caught up in the seasonal sentimentality, where Jesus is but one of a number of symbols meant to inspire kindness and good cheer: snowflakes, snowmen, sleigh rides, and the baby Jesus. Neither is Christ's birth a visual or emotional hook to convince us that we need to buy certain presents or gifts.

Rather, the birth of Christ is the long-awaited fulfill-ment of God's promises to His people, the beginning of the final exodus. Christ was born in a lowly estate, in the like-ness of sinful flesh, that He might redeem for His Father a people, that He might redeem for Himself a bride for whom

He laid down His life. The fulfilled promise of Christ is what the authors of the hymn saw running through the pages of Scripture. Our medieval forebears saw a thread that began in the earliest portions of the Scriptures in Israel's exodus, a thread that reappears in Israel's exodus from Babylon. It was a thread that began in these shadows that ultimately led to Christ's advent, to the One who would lead the Israel of God, the church, on the final exodus—the liberation out from under the tyranny of Satan, sin, and death.

Our forefathers ground this ancient hymn in the unfolding drama of God's revelation that culminates in the advent of Christ. It is certainly a hymn that the church should use to celebrate the Savior's birth. It is also one that should be upon the mouths of God's people throughout the year on every Lord's Day as Christ continues to lead us on the final exodus with the New Jerusalem as our destination, the new heavens and earth.

Let us therefore celebrate the birth of our Lord on God's appointed day by moving from the shadowlands of the Old Testament, the land of promises and types, into the fullness of the light of the revelation of Christ. At Christmas we must not forget to celebrate the season as our forefathers have—looking to Christ and longing for His second coming. Christmas should drive us to join hands with our ancestors and look eagerly to the horizon and sing with them, "Rejoice! Rejoice! Emmanuel shall come to thee, O Israel!" And one day, we will indeed be able to sing, "Rejoice! Rejoice! Emmanuel has come to thee, O Israel!"

Questions for Reflection

1. What other connections between the exodus and Christ's birth can you find in Scripture (hint: Ex. 1:15–16; Matt. 2:16)?

2. How is Israel's exodus like Jesus's early life immediately after His birth (hint: Matt. 2:15)?

3. Why do you think our medieval forefathers linked the exoduses from Egypt and Babylon to Christ's birth and second coming?

4. In what ways do we now live in exile from God's presence?

✳

THE MAGI AND THE KING

Now after Jesus was born in Bethlehem of Judea in the days of Herod the king, behold, wise men from the East came to Jerusalem, saying, "Where is He who has been born King of the Jews? For we have seen His star in the East and have come to worship Him."

When Herod the king heard this, he was troubled, and all Jerusalem with him. And when he had gathered all the chief priests and scribes of the people together, he inquired of them where the Christ was to be born.

So they said to him, "In Bethlehem of Judea, for thus it is written by the prophet:

'But you, Bethlehem, in the land of Judah,
Are not the least among the rulers of Judah;
For out of you shall come a Ruler
Who will shepherd My people Israel.'"

Then Herod, when he had secretly called the wise men, determined from them what time the star appeared. And he sent them to Bethlehem and said, "Go and search carefully for the young Child, and when you have found Him, bring back word to me, that I may come and worship Him also."

When they heard the king, they departed; and behold, the star which they had seen in the East went before them, till it came and stood over where the young Child was. When they saw the star, they rejoiced with exceedingly great joy. And when they had come into the house, they saw the young Child with Mary His mother, and fell down and worshiped Him.

And when they had opened their treasures, they presented gifts to Him: gold, frankincense, and myrrh.

Then, being divinely warned in a dream that they should not return to Herod, they departed for their own country another way.

—Matthew 2:1–12

———————————✳———————————

4

The Magi and the King

Popular Christmas depictions of Christ's birth feature three wise men coming from the East to worship the newly born King Jesus. Our culture has added an additional figure to the narrative through songs like "The Little Drummer Boy," which tells the story of a boy who was summoned by the wise men but who had no gift for Jesus. So the boy gave Jesus what he had: "I played my best for him," and "He smiled at me," says the song. Singers from Bing Crosby to Justin Bieber to Carrie Underwood to Bob Seger have sung this tune. Our culture has buried the biblical narrative of the wise men under the soundwaves of schmaltzy Christmas cheer.

While cultural renditions of the wise men (or magi) still persist in our time, the biblical account runs much deeper. Few of the popular images, depictions, or carols about the magi recognize that their visit was the catalyst for Herod's slaughter of the innocents in his effort to assassinate the newborn Christ, and that Herod's murderous plot motivated Joseph and Mary to flee to Egypt with their Son. These two facts alone should encourage us to take a closer look at the biblical account and refamiliarize ourselves with the magi's visit so that our culture's Christmas celebrations do not obscure important biblical truths that attend the birth of Jesus. We must not become captive to our culture's sentimentalism, which has slowly absorbed and changed the narrative of Christ's birth.

Gentiles and Geography

Two things that should create a cognitive dissonance are both the geographic details and the presence of gentiles in the biblical text. That Matthew wrote his gospel for a primarily Jewish audience is evident, for example, in his genealogies that explain that Jesus is both the Son of David and of Abraham (Matt. 1:1–17). Matthew's genealogy stamps his gospel with a definitive Jewish character. Against this backdrop the presence of gentile magi prominently stands out: "Behold, wise men from the East came to Jerusalem" (2:1). Why would wise men come from the East? From what country or region did they come? Moreover, what are wise men?

The fact that they came from the East signals that they were gentiles—Matthew does not identify them as Jews. Matthew also labels them as *wise men* (in the Greek, *magoi*, or literally *magi*). This is the same word from which we get the English words *magic* and *magician*. In fact, in the Greek translation of the Old Testament (the Septuagint), the book of Daniel places the magi among the Babylonian enchanters and sorcerers: "Then the king gave the command to call the magicians [*magous*], the astrologers, the sorcerers, and the Chaldeans to tell the king his dreams" (Dan. 2:2). Some biblical scholars suppose that, given their status as magi, they studied the stars and astrology. What were these wise men doing in Jerusalem? If these wise men came from the East, perhaps from a city like Babylon (near modern-day Baghdad), why would they make the thousand-mile journey to Jerusalem? According to Google, it would take 225 hours to walk from Baghdad to Jerusalem, which is more than eighteen days (assuming that they walked for twelve hours a day). The narrative of Christ's birth gives us some answers.

The magi arrived in Jerusalem and made their way to Herod's palace and inquired of the king, "Where is He who has been born King of the Jews? For we have seen His star in the East and have come to worship Him" (Matt. 2:2). Why did they make the long journey? They came to worship Jesus! But the stunning fact is, these are gentiles! King Herod was tucked away in his palace and could undoubtedly see the same star that pointed to the newborn King, and yet he did not seek Him. Gentiles from more than a thousand miles away made the long trek to worship Jesus.

Matthew powerfully captures the ironic, antithetical responses, but he does not merely point out Herod's impiety and the wise men's devotion. Matthew wanted his Jewish readers to know that Emmanuel, "God with us," was truly in their midst, and evidence of this was the fact that ancient biblical prophecies were being fulfilled. Isaiah prophesied of a time in the "latter days" when the nations would stream into Israel to worship Yahweh:

> Now it shall come to pass in the latter days
> That the mountain of the LORD's house
> Shall be established on the top of the mountains,
> And shall be exalted above the hills;
> And all nations shall flow to it.
> Many people shall come and say,

"Come, and let us go up to the mountain of the LORD,
To the house of the God of Jacob;
He will teach us His ways,
And we shall walk in His paths." (Isa. 2:2–3)

The psalmist also foretold of these events when he wrote:

The kings of Tarshish and of the isles
Will bring presents;
The kings of Sheba and Seba
Will offer gifts.
Yes, all kings shall fall down before Him;
All nations shall serve Him. (Ps. 72:10–11)

Both Isaiah and the psalmist foretold of a time when gentile royalty would stream into Israel to worship Yahweh, and the fulfillment of these promises was now unfolding. This is not to say that we see a complete fulfillment of the prophecies, as we await the consummation and conclusion of all things with the second advent of Christ and the final judgment—a day when every knee will bow and every tongue confess, in heaven and on earth and under the earth, that Jesus Christ is Lord, to the glory of God the Father (Phil. 2:10–11). But in this case, these cosmic events and the universal recognition of Christ's lordship by the whole world, Jew and gentile, have inauspicious beginnings with the visit of the wise men from the East. The appearance of the wise men from the East may seem insignificant, but even the greatest of events can have the smallest beginnings; such is the nature of the wise men's arrival.

When the wise men arrived, they told Herod, "We have seen His star in the East and have come to worship

Him" (Matt. 2:2), which undoubtedly raises this question: Is the knowledge of Christ revealed in the creation? In more specific theological terms, Can we know of the gospel from general revelation, from the stars? The simple answer is, no, we cannot. The only place we learn of Christ and His gospel is through special revelation or Scripture. So, then, how should we understand the wise men's claims about seeing Christ's star and learning of His birth through the creation?

While we cannot be absolutely certain, a likely scenario is that the wise men were exposed to Old Testament Scripture when God sent Israel into exile in Babylon. Recall that when Nebuchadnezzar conquered the Southern Kingdom of Judah, he besieged Jerusalem and brought some of the temple vessels of the house of God back with him. But we should note an important point in Daniel's narrative: "*And the Lord gave Jehoiakim king of Judah into his hand, with some of the articles of the house of God,* which he carried into the land of Shinar to the house of his god" (Dan. 1:2, emphasis added). While God exiled Israel for their sin, He was unfolding His plan of redemption through His invisible hand of providence. *God* sent the king and the vessels of the temple into Babylon, which means He was laying the groundwork for gentiles to learn of the gospel. We can safely assume that among the vessels of the temple were copies of God's Word. Recall during the reign of King Josiah when Hilkiah the high priest discovered a copy of the Book of the Law in the temple when they were cleaning it out (2 Kings 22:8–9). This means, at a minimum, there was likely a copy of the Torah—the first five books of the Old Testament—among the temple vessels.

Another possible source of the wise men's knowledge were the Israelites who served in Babylon's courts, such as Daniel, Hananiah, Mishael, and Azariah (also known by their Babylonian names as Belteshazzar, Shadrach, Meshach, and Abed-Nego) (Dan. 1:7). Babylonian officials singled out these young men to serve in the king's court because they were of royal descent, without blemish, of good appearance, and "skillful in all wisdom, endowed with knowledge, understanding learning, and competent" (v. 4 ESV). The words used to describe these young men reveal more than that they were smart and wise but that they understood and knew the Word of God. "God gave them knowledge and skill in all literature and wisdom; and Daniel had understanding in all visions and dreams" (v. 17), which is another way of saying he understood divine special revelation.

According to Hebrews, God "at various times and in various ways spoke in time past to the fathers by the prophets" (Heb. 1:1), and Daniel certainly was one of these prophets (Matt. 24:15). So, either by reading portions of the Old Testament or studying special revelation handed down from prophets like Daniel, the wise men may have learned of the Messiah. Another possibility is that God directly revealed the knowledge of His Son's birth to the wise men—just as He warned them not to return to Herod—which then spurred them to make the extensive expedition to worship Jesus (2:12).

But even then, the wise men's visit calls to mind other Old Testament passages of Scripture that would have reminded Matthew's readers of similar events. Recall the account of Balaam, the gentile pagan prophet who Balak, king of Beor, tried to hire to curse Israel. Rather than curse Israel, God had Balaam bless His people:

I see Him, but not now;
I behold Him, but not near;
A Star shall come out of Jacob;
A Scepter shall rise out of Israel. (Num. 24:17)

In other words, the gentile prophet-for-hire spoke of the coming Messiah, and his prophecy mentions both seeing Him from afar and beholding Him as a star, elements that resonate in Matthew's account. Matthew intends to show that Jesus is the Yes and Amen to all of God's promises (2 Cor. 1:20).

If we want to escape our cultural captivity, we must embrace the biblical text and reject the popular social versions of Christmas. One of the more troubling forms of our cultural captivity comes from allowing ourselves to use inaccurate visual images to communicate Christ's ministry. So-called sacred art as well as Hollywood's depictions of Christ only reflect a gaze into the long well of history where we see a reflection of ourselves. Sacred art and movies depict Jesus as a white Anglo-Saxon. When we look into the mirror and see someone who looks like us, it likely comforts and conveys to us the idea that we belong. Or in other cases, such portrayals send the message that the nations are not like Jesus and therefore do not belong. But the magi tell us something very different. Just as the magi are out of place, so gentiles who worship Jesus are out of place too. Paul clearly tells us gentiles that we are all aliens and strangers to the covenants of Israel (Eph. 2:19). But we who are far off have been brought near—Christ has torn down the wall of division, making out of the two one man (Eph. 2:14–15).

Only God's grace in Christ has enabled us outsiders, gentiles, to draw near to Christ—wild olive branches that have been lovingly and undeservingly grafted on to the tree of the Israel of God (Rom. 11:17). This is one of the chief points that Matthew presses in his birth account. Slowly but surely Matthew unveils the mystery of the gospel to his readers: Jesus is the King of the Jews *and* the gentiles! He unfurls the tapestry of God's love in Christ for Jews and gentiles in the opening verses of his gospel when he includes gentile women in Christ's genealogy: Ruth the Moabitess and Rahab the prostitute (Matt. 1:5). In one sense, the inclusion of these women is doubly unthinkable: not only are they women, virtually nonpersons in the first-century world, but they were gentiles.

Matthew highlights Christ's universal lordship when he includes the magi's visit and finally caps off his account with Christ's command to evangelize the nations: "Go therefore and make disciples of all the nations" (28:19). The culturally distorted message of Christmas tells us we belong, and strips out the message of the gospel—that we do not belong because we are sinners and gentiles. If we look upon the pages of Holy Writ, we see a different message: we do not belong but have been drawn in by God's mercy in Christ. We can therefore join the magi and the throng of gentiles as we flow into Zion to worship Christ, the King of Kings and Lord of Lords.

Government and Gifts

Matthew's account of the magi's visit is thick with irony because, as I noted from the outset, Herod and the magi have diametrically opposed responses. Herod dwelled in the heart of Israel, yet he was ignorant of Christ's birth. As king of the Jews, should Herod not have been aware of and anticipated and longed for His birth? Herod called the chief priests and scribes and consulted with them (Matt. 2:4). Unlike Herod, they were generally aware of the promise of Christ's birth and even quoted Micah 5:2 to Herod,

> But you, Bethlehem, in the land of Judah,
> Are not the least among the rulers of Judah;
> For out of you shall come a Ruler
> Who will shepherd My people Israel. (Matt. 2:6)

Herod took this information and secretly called the magi and asked them to search for the Messiah so that he too could worship him (vv. 7–8). Bethlehem was only five miles from Jerusalem. Why did Herod not go with the magi? The short answer is, because he was a liar and wanted to kill rather than worship Jesus. Jesus represented a threat to Herod's throne, and so he sought to assassinate Him. Herod's slaughter of the innocents hearkens back to Pharoah's effort to kill all the male children in Israel (Ex. 1:22).

The book of Revelation captures Herod's attempt to kill Jesus when John reports his vision of a woman clothed with the sun, the moon under her feet, and a crown of twelve stars, a representation of the nation of Israel. The woman was pregnant and crying out in birth pangs when a great red dragon with seven heads, ten horns, and seven crowns swept a third of the stars out of heaven and cast them to the earth, imagery that biblical scholars say speaks of Satan's revolt when he led angels to rebel against God. The dragon stood before the woman (Israel) as she was about to give birth so he could devour her child.

Who was this child? John tells us: "She bore a male Child who was to rule all nations with a rod of iron" (Rev. 12:5). This is Old Testament language reminiscent of Psalm 2's description of the Messiah: He would break the nations with a "rod of iron" and "dash them to pieces like a potter's vessel" (v. 9). John's vision informs us that Herod's blood-lust against Christ was nothing less than satanic. Yet, just as in the days of Moses God protected Israel's leader from Pharaoh's wrath, so John tells us that the "Child was caught up to God and His throne" (Rev. 12:5). In other words, God providentially protected His Son and sent Him into Egypt.

Herod's negative reaction stands out, but so does the response of the people. The scribes and chief priests made no effort to find Christ. You would think that if magi traveled over one thousand miles to worship the King of Israel, the Messiah, that even curiosity would motivate them to go with the magi. Again, the distance from Jerusalem to Bethlehem was a mere five miles, which would take less than two hours. After thousands of years and a myriad of prophecies, the religious leaders' lack of interest is stunning. But Herod and the religious leaders were not the only ones to respond. Matthew tells us that when Herod heard the news of the birth of Christ, "he was troubled, and all Jerusalem with him" (Matt. 2:3). Even the people of Jerusalem were troubled by the news of Christ's birth rather than being filled with joy.

These negative reactions stand in stark contrast to the gentile magi who "fell down and worshiped" Jesus (Matt. 2:11). Moreover, the magi brought Jesus costly gifts such as gold, which even by today's standards is still expensive. Frankincense is a valuable resin used in perfumes and mentioned in a number of Old Testament passages:

> The multitude of camels shall cover your land,
> The dromedaries of Midian and Ephah;
> All those from Sheba shall come;
> They shall bring gold and incense,
> And they shall proclaim the praises of the LORD.
>   (Isa. 60:6; see also Song 4:14; Jer. 6:20)

Myrrh was another valuable resin used in perfumes and medicines. All these things were gifts fit for royalty, but more importantly they reflect the dispositions of the hearts of the magi. Unlike Herod, the scribes, the chief priests, or the people of Jerusalem, these gentile dogs, strangers and aliens to the covenants and promises, fell on their faces and worshiped Christ.

Herein lies another point where we must seek to escape our cultural captivity. Our culture tells us that we give gifts at Christmas because the magi brought gifts to Jesus. But notice that the wise men did not give gifts to each other or to anyone else but only to Jesus. Yet how much do we echo the culture's idea that Christmas is about giving gifts to each other? If the magi's gifts tell us anything, then Christmas should be first and foremost about giving gifts to Christ. While we can manifest a spirit of charity and kindness and give gifts to others, the Bible calls us to join the magi in giving costly gifts to Christ and bowing before Him and worshiping. As the book of Hebrews exhorts us: "There-fore by Him let us continually offer the sacrifice of praise to God, that is, the fruit of our lips, giving thanks to His name" (13:15). When we contemplate the birth of Christ, that we were strangers and aliens to the covenants and promises but have been drawn near through God's grace in Christ, praise and thanksgiving should fill our hearts and should overflow in acts of love and worship to our triune God.

But once again, we must remember that the only way we can and will render our lives unto God as living sacrifices is if we are first the recipients of God's love in Christ. Remember the message of the angels to the shep-herds watching their flocks by night: "Glory to God in the highest, and on earth peace among those with whom he is pleased" (Luke 2:14 ESV). Only by God's grace did these gentile magi see through the fog and darkness of their idolatry and find their way to worship Jesus. God divinely and supernaturally guided them by a star and by revealing the gospel to them, either through Old Testament Scrip-ture or through revelatory visions (Matt. 2:12). We must pray, therefore, that God would shower us in His grace in Christ so that we too will prostrate our hearts before Jesus, the King of Kings and Lord of Lords.

Conclusion

Our unbelieving culture will use any and every possible means to smother the gospel. In this case, the culture takes elements of the gospel, such as the magi and their gifts, and dilutes their biblical content until it has created a vaccine. Unbelievers and even Christians inject the culture with the diluted form of the Christmas message, and people then become immune to it. The magi worshiping God incarnate becomes a Christmas carol, a little boy playing his drum for Jesus as the Savior gives him a passing smile. The birth narrative becomes a sentimental expression of holiday cheer rather than the recognition that the infant nestled in Mary's arms would one day don a crown of thorns and be crucified so that we, aliens and strangers to the covenants and promises of God, would have salvation. Rejoice that you have been brought near to Christ by His blood. With the gentile wise men, bow down and worship Christ, the King of Kings and Lord of Lords. Christmas should always remind us that though we did not belong, by God's grace we have been brought in and made citizens of heaven and coheirs with Christ, the Son of God.

Questions for Reflection

1. Can you think of other ways the culture tries to dilute the message of Christ's birth?

2. How should our gentile "outsider" status inform our stance toward people outside the church?

3. Why should we not make visual representations of Jesus? How do they make us feel like we belong to God's people? How might they make others feel like they do not belong to God's people?

4. How do the magi reveal the sovereign grace of God in salvation?

SIMEON'S PRAYER

Now when the days of her purification according to the law of Moses were completed, they brought Him to Jerusalem to present Him to the Lord (as it is written in the law of the Lord, "Every male who opens the womb shall be called holy to the LORD"), and to offer a sacrifice according to what is said in the law of the Lord, "A pair of turtledoves or two young pigeons."

And behold, there was a man in Jerusalem whose name was Simeon, and this man was just and devout, waiting for the Consolation of Israel, and the Holy Spirit was upon him. And it had been revealed to him by the Holy Spirit that he would not see death before he had seen the Lord's Christ. So he came by the Spirit into the temple. And when the parents brought in the Child Jesus, to do for Him according to the custom of the law, he took Him up in his arms and blessed God and said:

"Lord, now You are letting Your servant depart in peace,
According to Your word;
For my eyes have seen Your salvation
Which You have prepared before the face of all peoples,
A light to bring revelation to the Gentiles,
And the glory of Your people Israel."

And Joseph and His mother marveled at those things which were spoken of Him. Then Simeon blessed them, and said to Mary His mother, "Behold, this Child is destined for the fall and rising of many in Israel, and for a sign which will be spoken against (yes, a sword will pierce through your own soul also), that the thoughts of many hearts may be revealed."

Now there was one, Anna, a prophetess, the daughter of Phanuel, of the tribe of Asher. She was of a great age, and had lived with a husband seven years from her virginity; and this woman was a widow of about eighty-four years, who did not depart from the temple, but served God with fastings and prayers night and day. And coming in that instant she gave thanks to the Lord, and spoke of Him to all those who looked for redemption in Jerusalem.

So when they had performed all things according to the law of the Lord, they returned to Galilee, to their own city, Nazareth. And the Child grew and became strong in spirit, filled with wisdom; and the grace of God was upon Him.

—Luke 2:22–40

———————————✳———————————

5

Simeon's Prayer

My theology professor's face was beet red, and he yelled at me, "The God of the Old Testament is one of wrath, don't you see? The God of the New Testament is one of love!" I sunk down in my seat and wished a hole would open in the floor to allow me to escape, but I sat there nonetheless as my professor continued to berate me. Never mind the fact that he was angrily bellowing at me because I supposedly misunderstood God's love. The irony of the moment was thick as he angrily yelled at me about the love of God, but the sentiment is common among many in the church.

A superficial reading of the Old Testament might lead some to a similar conclusion. God sits atop Mount Sinai shrouded in dark, thunderous clouds, whereas the New Testament seemingly presents a very different picture, especially as we reflect upon Christ's birth narrative. The dark clouds of Sinai dissipate and leave us with a meek and lowly infant. But when we drill down into Luke's account of Simeon's encounter with the infant Savior (traditionally called the Nunc Dimittis, meaning "Now you are letting," taken from the words of Simeon's prayer from the Latin Bible), we see a perfect wedding between the Old and New Testaments: we worship one God, there is one gospel, and there is one hope of salvation.

Simeon's encounter with the infant Christ reveals that

God has not changed from one testament to the next—He has, is, and will forever remain the same. The triune God has always intended to focus our attention upon the revelation of Christ and His gospel. Only by looking at the big picture through Simeon's prayer will we have a greater understanding of these truths so that we will join Simeon in prayer and eagerly await the return of Christ, the Consolation of Israel.

Christ's Appearance in the Temple

All too often when we read the Bible, we fail to note small details and instead walk away with a thin reading of Scripture. There is a sense in which we read Scripture and only see it as if it were flat—two dimensions—unaware that there is a third dimension that adds greater depth and detail. In this particular case, one of the significant but often missed details is the location of Simeon's prayer—the temple. Recall the importance of the temple in the Old Testament. God led Israel out of Egypt through the pillar of cloud by day and fire by night. The glory-cloud presence of God came to rest atop Sinai in thick clouds of darkness attended by peels of thunder and flashes of lightning. God eventually took up residence in the desert tabernacle and later in Solomon's temple. The temple was God's dwelling place in the midst of His people.

With this in mind, note where Luke places the unfolding events of Christ's dedication: "And it had been revealed to [Simeon] by the Holy Spirit that he would not see death before he had seen the Lord's Christ. So he came by the Spirit into the temple" (Luke 2:26–27). Likewise, another godly saint was present in the temple: "[Anna] did not depart from the temple, but served God with fastings and prayers night and day" (v. 37). Simeon and Anna both lingered in the temple because this was the center of God's presence among His people, and He blessed their faithful patience.

God in the flesh appeared in the temple carried by His faithful parents. God once again visited His people in the temple, but this time it was not in a pillar of fire, dark clouds, or lightning. Neither did God strike dead Mary, Joseph, or Simeon for touching Him as He did Uzzah for touching the ark, which was merely God's throne. Nor did God strike dead Anna for looking upon Jesus, God in the flesh, though she was not a priest.

In fact, there is something utterly remarkable about Christ's presence—He is in His temple, but He is *outside* the holy of holies! Christ's appearance in the temple has roots that run deep into Israel's covenantal history, as all of the Old Testament markers are present—sacrifices, the temple, and God's people worshiping Him. But God's presence is different. He is the same God of Sinai, but He has condescended to His people meek and lowly in the form of a humble servant, a child.

At first glance, we might think this fits the mold of the common, mistaken caricature of the Old Testament God versus the New Testament God. Yet, that Christ comes into the temple, God in the flesh but as a child, is not the antithesis of the Old Testament but is its very fulfillment. No longer does Eve await the birth of her Seed, the One who will crush the head of the serpent. Abraham awaited the day of Christ, the advent of his Seed, and he could see it from afar, but now that day was here (John 8:56). David waited for the birth of his greater Son and Lord, the One who would sit on his throne to rule Israel, and now that day had dawned (2 Sam. 7:12–16).

God's people had waited for ages, but their waiting was now over. Simeon's life of patient, faithful waiting is a microcosm of all the hopes of God's saints in ages past. Simeon was old but could now know the hope of the Aaronic blessing—the face of God had shone upon Simeon in the face of Christ—and he could now die in peace knowing that God was faithful to His covenant promises. When we contemplate the birth of Christ, does the same peace fall upon our hearts? Do we mistakenly think that God was angry in the Old Testament and that a radical change took place, where a different god stepped onto the stage of redemptive history? Or perhaps do we think that God had a change of heart and decided to amend His wrathful ways and instead show His people patience, kindness, and love? Or do we instead rightly bow our hearts before the infant Christ and recognize that the same God of Sinai sent His only begotten Son to save us as He promised? The light of God's faithfulness in Christ should fill our hearts and dispel the dark clouds of doubt and error about who God is.

Christ's Faithfulness

God's faithfulness in Christ appears throughout this passage in ways that we might not immediately see. God's fidelity is emphasized in the opening words of Simeon's prayer: "Lord, now You are letting Your servant depart in peace, *according*

to Your word" (Luke 2:29, emphasis added). God fulfilled
His covenant promises to Adam and Eve, Abraham, Isaac,
Jacob, David, and to all His people. This is why the apostle
Paul writes that all the promises of God find their Amen in
Christ (2 Cor. 1:20). But do you see the regular, rhythmic
drumbeat that Luke plays throughout this passage?

> Now when the days of her purification *according
> to the law of Moses* were completed, they brought
> Him to Jerusalem to present Him to the Lord (*as it
> is written in the law of the Lord*, "Every male who
> opens the womb shall be called holy to the LORD"),
> and to offer a sacrifice *according to what is said in the
> law of the Lord*, "A pair of turtledoves or two young
> pigeons.'…
>
> So when they had performed all things *according
> to the law of the Lord*, they returned to Galilee, to
> their own city, Nazareth. (Luke 2:22–24, 39, empha-
> sis added)

Luke connects Mary and Joseph's actions to the fulfillment of the law four times, which highlights at least two
things. First, it underscores Mary and Joseph's piety and
devotion to the Lord. In contrast to Adam and Eve's trans-
gression of His covenantal command not to eat from the
Tree of the Knowledge of Good and Evil (Gen. 2:16–17),
Mary and Joseph's repeated obedience stands out. Luke,
however, does not want us to focus upon Mary and Joseph's
obedience. Rather, second, Luke dresses the infant Christ
in His robe of righteousness to show that, even in His
infancy, Jesus was fulfilling His heavenly Father's holy law.
Luke does not dwell on Mary's fidelity or any purported

role that Roman Catholics erroneously assign to her. Every one of Mary and Joseph's actions anticipate Christ's words to John the Baptist when He submitted to John's baptism of repentance: "Permit it to be so now, for thus it is fitting for us to fulfill all righteousness" (Matt. 3:15).

Simeon did not rejoice in Mary's faithfulness but in God's faithfulness in Christ: "For my eyes have seen Your salvation which You have prepared before the face of all peoples" (Luke 2:30–31). God was fulfilling His promises to save His people in accordance with His word and numerous Old Testament promises. In this vein, it is significant that Luke records that God revealed to Simeon that He would behold "the Lord's Christ" (v. 26). *Christ* is a word that is very familiar to us given how prevalent the name Jesus Christ is within and without the church. Sometimes I get the impression that people invoke the two parts of the Savior's name as if *Christ* were his family name rather than an official title. *Christ* is the English transliteration of the Greek term *christos*, which is a translation of the Hebrew term *meshiach*, which means "anointed." This is the term that the psalmist famously invokes in Psalm 2:

> The kings of the earth set themselves,
> And the rulers take counsel together,
> Against the LORD and against His Anointed. (v. 2)

The long-awaited anointed Servant of God was now here, and this is why Simeon rejoiced and knew that he could die in peace. He could also personally witness the Messiah's faithfulness—the infant was fully God, but He was also fully man. Simeon was witnessing the righteous Man of Psalm 1 as He faithfully obeyed His Father's will—so that He would be the perfectly righteous Messiah to ascend David's throne—and the God-man of Psalm 2. The God of Sinai came down from His holy mountain because His people were incapable of coming up to Him. He graciously came out of the holy of holies so that we could enter in by the faithfulness of His Son.

Christ, Our Only Hope

In Simeon's encounter with the infant Christ, there is a sense in which the Old Testament never leaves the scene. As we have noted, this passage is replete with Old Testament imagery and activity. Yes, God has come humbly, meekly, and lowly, which is different from His Old Testament revelations. But recall how God's Old Testament revelation always produced division. When God revealed visions and dreams to Joseph and then Joseph disclosed those dreams to his father and brothers, they were angered— his brothers scorned his dreams and rejected him by selling him into slavery. God gave His revelation, and it divided the people. The Israelites regularly spurned Moses's leadership—Korah and his sons rebelled against the Lord (Num. 16:1–40). God vindicated Moses and judged Korah—the earth swallowed him and his family whole.

The author of the letter to the Hebrews succinctly captures this truth when he writes,

> For the word of God is living and powerful, and sharper than any two-edged sword, piercing even to the division of soul and spirit, and of joints and marrow, and is a discerner of the thoughts and intents of the heart. And there is no creature hidden from His

sight, but all things are naked and open to the eyes of
Him to whom we must give account. (Heb. 4:12–13)

God's word and revelation are double-edged. His word is
double-edged in the Old Testament; His word is double-
edged in the New Testament, whether His incarnate or
written word.

In continuity with the Old Testament, the two-edged
nature of God's revelation unfolds here in Simeon's words
to Mary: "Behold, this Child is destined for the fall and
rising of many in Israel" (Luke 2:34). This truth would
unfold throughout Christ's ministry, as many Israelites
would repent and believe, but many would instead revile
and reject Christ. Mary knew this because she prayed in
her Magnificat,

He has put down the mighty from their thrones,
And exalted the lowly.
He has filled the hungry with good things,
And the rich He has sent away empty. (1:52–53)

Herod sought to kill Jesus, whereas the magi came to
worship Him—rejection and acceptance, judgment and
salvation (Matt. 2:1–12). The double-edged pattern unfolded
in Christ's crucifixion, as one thief reviled Christ as He
hung suffering on the cross and the other thief believed in
Jesus, died, and went to paradise with Christ that very day
(Luke 23:43).

The twofold purpose of revelation continues to unfold
in the preaching ministry of the church, as Paul himself was acutely aware of the burden that preachers carry
upon their shoulders: "For we are to God the fragrance of
Christ among those who are being saved and among those

who are perishing. To the one we are the aroma of death leading to death, and to the other the aroma of life leading to life. And who is sufficient for these things?" (2 Cor. 2:15–16). Not everyone embraces the light of the gospel. Left to ourselves, we flee from the light and try to hide in the darkness and shadows of our sin lest the light expose us. Only by God's grace in Christ do we come out of the darkness and enter the light of the gospel. This is the truth of Christmas that our culture never touts, but this is the truth we must remember so that we will seek shelter in the embassy of Christ's gospel.

But Simeon also had specific words for Mary: "A sword will pierce through your own soul also" (Luke 2:35). We get the smallest of glimpses into Mary's life: she would stand on the sidelines and watch her Son carry out His ministry in obedience to His heavenly Father. She would know the rejection of her own people. She would see her Son despised, insulted, and ultimately crucified. One of the most difficult things for a parent to bear is to watch her child suffer, knowing that she is powerless to help, heal, or give hope. The words of one contemporary lamentation written by Ann Weems on the death of Christ likely captures Mary's thoughts as she would one day stand at the foot of the cross in tears:

> They killed him
> whom you gave to me.
> They killed him
> without a thought
> for justice or mercy,

and I sit now in darkness
hosannas stuck in my throat…

God, therefore, was warning Mary of her great pain and suffering to come, but He did not leave her without hope. When Mary and Joseph brought the infant Savior to the temple that day, they met Simeon, who was "waiting for the Consolation of Israel" (Luke 2:25), and he expressed this when he prayed to God in the hearing of Mary and Joseph that God had allowed him to see His salvation (v. 30). I suspect that watching her Son die on the cross was a crushing blow for Mary, but that perhaps her mind drifted back to this day in the temple and her encounter with Simeon—his words of foretold suffering echoed in her memory, but they were also wrapped in hope.

Christ was Simeon's only hope, and this is why he found consolation, salvation, and confidence in Jesus, the Christ. As we behold the infant Christ through the eyes of faith, we too must not lose sight of this same hope. The only hope we have in the face of our sin and impending judgment is to seek shelter in Christ. We must pray that God would give us eyes of faith by His grace so that we would come out of the darkness and step into the light of the gospel. While Christ's sword of truth will undoubtedly cut us, and cut us deeply, He does not wield this sword unto judgment but unto life. The sword of His gospel truth is not the soldier's blade that cleaves and hacks but the surgeon's scalpel that removes our sinful hearts of stone so that He can heal us and give us hearts of flesh. While such a surgery is at times painful—Christ bids us to take up our crosses and follow Him, after all—He nevertheless imparts life, and life eternal.

Conclusion

God does not change—He is not the angry God of the Old Testament and the loving God of the New. If we pit the Old against the New Testament, we render the message of the gospel meaningless. Only when we recognize that we too stand at the foot of Sinai and cannot ascend the mountain because of God's holiness and wrath and because of our sin can we fully appreciate His incarnation—that He was willing to send His Son, to descend from Sinai's fiery heights, to emerge from behind the veil of the holy of holies, to take the form of a servant, and to be born as a man—a child humble, meek, and lowly. Only against the backdrop of the Old Testament can we understand and appreciate Christ's perfect fulfillment of the law in our place, even in His infancy. Only through a thorough reading of Scripture—both Old and New Testaments—can we appreciate the significance of Christ's birth and the reason for Simeon's joy, hope, and peace. Our prayer should be that God would grant us the faith of Simeon as we too await the Consolation of Israel. When Christ returns, we will be able to join with Simeon and say,

> For my eyes have seen Your salvation
> Which You have prepared before the face of all
>   peoples,
> A light to bring revelation to the Gentiles,
> And the glory of Your people Israel. (Luke 2:30–32)

Questions for Reflection

1. Why is the temple such an important feature in Simeon's encounter with the infant Christ?

2. In what way was Christ fulfilling the law on our behalf, even in His infancy?

3. What is the significance that God in the flesh appears outside of the holy of holies?

4. Has God changed from the Old to the New Testament, a God of wrath versus a God of love?

Conclusion

The Christmas holiday season is undoubtedly a joyous time of year, but we should always be on guard lest we allow our culture to rob us of the hope of the gospel. In the midst of all this seasonal joy, we should regularly immerse ourselves in the Scriptures to ensure that we do not forget what the birth of Christ is all about. Regardless of the holiday, we do not want our culture to drown out the message of the gospel. We do not want to allow our culture's festivities to dilute biblical truth or displace Christ from Christmas. When we think of the angel's message to Mary, we should join her in worshiping our triune God for His faithfulness throughout the ages. The announcement the angels made to the shepherds should cause us to rejoice in the gospel of salvation and God's grace and that His peace rests upon those with whom He is pleased (Luke 2:14 ESV).

Looking upon the birth of Christ in the pages of Scripture through the eyes of faith should remind us that God delivered His people from Egypt and returned Israel to the promised land from Babylon, and that Christ will return to lead us on the final exodus. With our ancestors from ages past, we should rise and sing, "Rejoice! Rejoice! Emmanuel shall come to thee, O Israel," even if we presently dwell in lonely exile from New Jerusalem. Even though the world touts Christmas as a time of peace, unity, and belonging, we should remember that we are like the gentile magi—we did not belong among God's people, but because of God's grace and mercy, He has made us, who were strangers and aliens to God's covenants, fellow citizens and heirs with the people of God. We who were once not a people are now a people—indeed, sons of the living God—because of God's grace in Christ.

In the end, Christmas should be a time of year that reminds us that God is the same yesterday, today, and tomorrow—He is the same God of the Old and New Testaments—and because of His constancy, fidelity, and immutability, we can look upon the birth of Christ and know that one day we will behold God's face in the face of Christ the way that Simeon did on that august day in the temple. Each Lord's Day, and especially at Christmas, we can reflect upon the birth of Christ and eagerly anticipate, saying with Simeon, "My eyes have seen Your salvation which you have prepared before the face of all peoples" (Luke 2:30–31)!

Works Consulted

Beale, G. K. *The Book of Revelation*. New International Greek Testament Commentary. Grand Rapids: Eerdmans, 1998.

Beale, G. K., and D. A. Carson, eds. *Commentary on the New Testament Use of the Old Testament*. Grand Rapids: Baker Academic, 2007.

Bock, Darrell. *Luke*. 2 volumes. Baker Exegetical Commentary on the New Testament. Grand Rapids: Baker, 1996.

Carson, D. A. *Matthew: Chapters 1–12*. Volume 1. Expositor's Bible Commentary. Grand Rapids: Zondervan, 1995.

Hagner, Donald. *Matthew: 1–13*. Volume 33a. Word Biblical Commentary. Nashville, Tenn.: Thomas Nelson, 1993.

Weems, Ann. *Psalms of Lament*. Louisville, Ky.: Westminster John Knox Press, 1995.